REFERENCES TO SALVADOR DALÍ MAKE ME HOT

José Rivera

BROADWAY PLAY PUBLISHING INC
224 E 62nd St, NY NY 10065
212 772-8334 fax: 212 772-8358
BroadwayPlayPub.com

First printing: October 2001
this printing, revised: November 2012
I S B N: 978-0-88145-200-6

Book design: Marie Donovan
Typeface: Palatino
Printed and bound in the U S A

REFERENCES TO SALVADOR DALÍ MAKE ME
HOT was developed with the assistance of the Mark
Taper Forum (Gordon Davidson, Artistic Director), the
Ensemble Studio Theater West (Garrett Brown, Artistic
Director), The Joseph Papp Public Theater (George C
Wolfe, Producer), the Relentless Theater Company
(Olivia Honegger, Artistic Director), Duke University,
South Coast Repertory (David Emmes and Martin
Benson, Artistic Directors), and Playwrights' Center of
Minneapolis.

REFERENCES TO SALVADOR DALÍ MAKE ME
HOT received its world premiere on 28 January 2000
at South Coast Repertory (David Emmes, Producing
Artistic Director; Martin Benson, Artistic Director;
Pacific Life Foundation was the honorary associate
producer). The cast and creative contributors were as
follows:

MOON	Robert Montano
COYOTE	Victor Mack
CAT	Svetlana Efremova
MARTIN	Wells Rosales
GABRIELA	Ana Ortiz
BENITO	Robert Montano
Director	Juliette Carrillo
Set design	Monica Raya
Lighting design	Geoff Korf
Costume design	Meg Neville
Sound design & original music	Mitch Greenhill
Dramaturg	John Glore
Stage manager	Randall K Lum

REFERENCES TO SALVADOR DALÍ MAKE ME
HOT received its New York premiere on 11 April
2001 at the Joseph Papp Public Theater/ New York
Shakespeare Festival (George C Wolfe, Producer; Fran
Reiter, Executive Director; Rosemarie Tichler, Artistic
Producer). The cast and creative contributors were
as follows:

MOON .... Michael Lombard
GABRIELA .... Rosie Perez
COYOTE..Kevin Jackson
CAT .... Kristine Nielsen
MARTIN .... Carlo Alban
BENITO.. John Ortiz

Director..Jo Bonney
Set design.. Neil Patel
Lighting design ....David Weiner
Costume design...Clint E B Ramos
Sound design............Donald DiNociola & Obadiah Eaves
Original music..Carlos Valdez
Dramaturg ....John Dias
Stage manager.. Mike Schleifer

Special thanks to Julia Edwards, Jo Bonney, John Ortiz, Camilia Sanes, Jeff Storer, Jessica Hecht, Jerry Patch, John Dias, Mervin P Antonio, Zannie Voss, Michele Vazquez, Maricela Ochoa, Iona Brindle, Ruth Livier, Oscar Arguello, Jesus Mendoza, Stefan Olmsted, Adam Rosenblatt, Dana Parker Bennison, Imoh Ime Essien, Adam Saunders, Joel McCauley Jr, Chris Schussler, Laura K Lewis, Julio Monge, Tony Torn, Danyon Davis, Carlo Alban, Timothy Huang, Shirley Fishman, Richard Coca, Sol Castillo, Sue Karutz, John Iacovelli, Doc Ballard, Nephelie Andonyadis, Amy Colon, Rachel Malkenhorst, Tom Lenoci, Wendy Johnson, Alex Fernandez and Megan Monaghan.

CHARACTERS & SETTING

MOON, *the moon in the sky,* GABRIELA's *friend (can double as* BENITO)
COYOTE, *a wild one*
CAT, *a fat one,* GABRIELA's *pet*
MARTIN, *a Latino of fourteen,* GABRIELA's *neighbor*
GABRIELA, *a Latina, late twenties, an Army housewife*
BENITO, *a Latino, early thirties,* GABRIELA's *husband, a soldier*

Time: Shortly after the Persian Gulf War

Place: Barstow, California

ACT ONE
GABRIELA's backyard. Night

ACT TWO
GABRIELA's kitchen. 7 A M

Intermission

ACT THREE
GABRIELA's bedroom. Night

ACT FOUR
GABRIELA's backyard. 7 A M

"And I'll sleep at your feet,
to watch over your dreams."
—BLOOD WEDDING

The play is dedicated to my soldier-brothers,
Julio, Charlie, Tony, and Hector.

ACT ONE

(Barstow, California. Night.)

(A cement-covered backyard. Cactus. Birds-of-paradise. Large spiny-edged aloe.)

(A wooden fence upstage. Beyond is the desert surrounded by low, barren mountains.)

(The MOON, *standing on an old refrigerator, plays the violin: something lush and sentimental.)*

(A female CAT *and a male* COYOTE *regard each other warily.)*

(The COYOTE *howls.)*

COYOTE: You don't trust me.

CAT: You're transparent.

COYOTE: You smell like soap.

CAT: You smell like shit.

COYOTE: Shit's natural. Remember natural?

CAT: You're full of secrets and worms.

COYOTE: You don't even know
what fresh blood tastes like!

CAT: Hunted!

COYOTE: Brainwashed!

CAT: Unloved!

(The COYOTE *howls with laughter.)*

COYOTE: Unloved? I'm free! I am myself!

CAT: Deluded.

COYOTE: And how do I keep my freedom?
I don't worry about their love—
their clinging, petting, hurtful...

CAT: Ay, jealous too!

COYOTE: Love with chains and flea collars attached.
Love with no purpose to it,
no reproduction, no passion.
Love predicated on obedience.
Love with violence implied.

CAT: You have no idea how good it is.

COYOTE: You think everything they do is good.
Have you seen what they've done to my desert?
The way the mountains
are so nicely carved up—
oh, such beautiful scars!—
oh, the pretty bomb craters!—
those sexy switchblade cuts
in the flesh of the land!
What kind of drugs
do they put in your food?

CAT: How cold does it get at night, Coyote?
How hard is that desert mattress?
What's in that darkness?
What's it like to live
in a world full of enemies?

COYOTE: Fun. Easy.

CAT: And the reason for the terror
in your eyes...?

COYOTE: That's lethal energy you see in my eyes, Cat.

CAT: Scavenger energy.

COYOTE: A hunter's gaze.

CAT: Bone-picker energy.
You let the real hunters
do the killing:
let cars do the killing.
Then you come along,
tail between your legs,
sniffing around for the leftovers,
all weasely and cautious,
licking up the cold blood
and competing with the flies
for the juicy bits.

COYOTE: Disinformation!

CAT: Oh, such honor.
Nature at its best.
Majestic, awesome nature!

COYOTE: You wouldn't survive a day—

CAT: You're not even smart enough
to be a dog.
What exactly are you?
Half-rat? Half-mole?

COYOTE: Not a single cold night!

CAT: Poor me, with a home,
protection from the sun,
good eats, lots of toys:
Gabriela gives me everything.

COYOTE: Toys and regular meals
have made you fat.
Blunted your instincts.
Why don't you come out with me?
Right now: do what I do for one night.
No home, no petting,
no flea collar, no place to hide.
You couldn't do it, could you?

CAT: I don't have to prove a—

COYOTE: Prove it to yourself.
Twenty-four hours in the wild.
I'll take you to the desert.
I'll take you hunting—
lots of prey, natural enemies to dodge—
you'll learn to look
at your precious Gabriela
from a real animal's point of view.

CAT: I take one step out of this yard,
you and your little posse gang-attacks me.

COYOTE: You have my word.

CAT: *(Sizing him up)*
Bet you'd love that...eating me.
Tasting my round, warm meat.
Domesticity has made my fatty parts
soft, easy, and wet with juice.
I can see the saliva forming in your mouth
right now.

COYOTE: That all you see?

CAT: After you've swallowed my
moist outer layers—
you can chew my heart muscles
and give your jaws a real workout.
Take you all night to eat my thighs.

COYOTE: Saliva's dripping down
and something else is coming up.

CAT: Not really.

COYOTE: Oh yeah.

CAT: What a pig!

COYOTE: You ain't never been laid
by a wild animal, have you?

CAT: Is that what all this has been about?

COYOTE: Like you didn't know!

CAT: Barbarian!

COYOTE: In the wild we really know how to love.
In the wild we do it under the savage sky,
get dirt in our eyes,
wet the ground with our funky juice.
It's not pretty but it's effective.
You scream so hard your ancestors hear you.
It's not even sex, it's beyond sex,
beyond bodies, come on, Cat,
animal on animal.
I'll knock you around so hard
all nine of your lives will have orgasms.

CAT: ...All nine?

COYOTE: Then you'll bear little coyote-cats—
tough mutant sons-of-bitches
who love the taste of blood
and the chase and the moonlit night.

CAT: I can't do that—I'm fixed.

COYOTE: Fixed? Fixed?
Oh, the beautiful English language!

CAT: Answer is No!

COYOTE: Aw, I wasn't going to beg!
This is me begging!
(He begs for sex. He's shameless.)

CAT: Of course you're begging.
You know what's in store for you.
Nobody loves like a house cat.

COYOTE: What do I have to say?
What do I have to promise?

CAT: Let me see.

COYOTE: A little lick? A sniff?
Mind if I wet the edge
of my tongue with your—?

CAT: What about some information?
What happened to Pinkie Garcia?

COYOTE: Pinkie—who?

CAT: Neighbor. Male.
long tail, weakness for grasshoppers.

COYOTE: Don't know a thing about that...

CAT: Pinkie's been missing two days, Coyote.

COYOTE: Why are you asking me?

CAT: What about Climber Rodriguez?
Missing a week! Any clues?

COYOTE: You watch that tone of voice!

CAT: All the neighbor cats've been disappearing
beginning with the first day
of your arrival in Barstow.
Making dirty war on my people!

(*The* COYOTE *grabs the* CAT.)

COYOTE: (*Laughing*)
You hate war, huh?
War makes you comfortable, Cat.

(*A 14-year-old Latino boy,* MARTIN *appears at the fence. He looks at the yard through a telescope.*)

(*The* MOON *notices* MARTIN, *snickers.*)

MOON: Aw, look at the little perv—
back for more...

MARTIN: She better be so naked tonight!
(*Seeing the* COYOTE)
A coyote! And me without a weapon!

(MARTIN's *presence gets the* CAT's *attention.*)

CAT: You better go before that boy
finds a weapon.

COYOTE: No way I'm leaving without you.

(The COYOTE *continues to beg for sex.)*

(The CAT *refuses.)*

MOON: *(To* MARTIN*)*
Give it up, little boy,
she's outta your league.

MARTIN: But Gabriela's my religion, Moon.
My altered state of grace.
I look at her ass and I hallucinate.
I'm all falling into her like I'm dying
and her body is the grave
and I got buried between her loins
and get to spend eternity
swimming in her
like a warm, creamy, gooey bath!
But what if I was born too late?
I'll be forever in exile.
Forced to watch her from a distance
and contemplate what never
could have been.

MOON: You want me to kick your ass?

(The back door opens.)

*(*GABRIELA, *a Latina of 27, wearing sweatshirt and
sweatpants, rushes into the yard.* GABRIELA *holds a
.9-millimeter pistol.)*

GABRIELA: Enemies! Enemies!

COYOTE: *(Seeing the weapon)*
Holy God!
(He hides.)

GABRIELA: Who's out here?
I'll shoot.

CAT: Just me, Gabriela!

GABRIELA: I heard voices.

CAT: Put the weapon down, *nena*,
and go back inside
before you kill us all.

GABRIELA: Who's out here with you?
Vampires? Are there vampires?

COYOTE: *(To CAT)*
Don't tell her about me, please—

GABRIELA: They say vampires are buying
up houses all over Barstow.
They say vampires are well organized.
They've filed down their teeth.
They smile without fear of detection.
They gain your trust.
You invite them over for barbecues.
You go to movies together.
You cuddle during the scary bits.
You unzip their flies.
Then you close your eyes
and they sink their miniature fangs
into your unprotected psyches
and drain the blood from your mind
until you're One Of Them.

CAT: Really, Gabriela, you need to get laid.

GABRIELA: Ay, don't remind me!

CAT: When does Benito get back from the field?

GABRIELA: I heard voices.
That's voices—plural.

CAT: *(A glance at the COYOTE)*
Eh—no—it's just me—and the moon.

(The MOON laughs.)

MOON: *Ay Dios*, those pajamas!

GABRIELA: The moon? The distant moon?

COYOTE: *(Sotto voce)*
Bless you, gentle, sexy Cat!

GABRIELA: Ay! I haven't had a lover's eyes
to look into for months.
I've been looking up
at the night sky instead,
watching the watchful moon.
Noticing the stars and galaxies.
Before you're born, I wonder,
as you looked around,
and took inventory of the womb...
did it look like this?
Did you see the moon and stars in there?
Floating bits of fire—maybe the nutrients from your
mother's bloodstream—
looking like constellations
against the deep, deep black
of your mother's night sky?
What do you say, Moon?
What's the good word tonight?

MOON: It's a jungle down there.

GABRIELA: I knew it.
That's why I have this!

(GABRIELA *fires a shot in the air.)*

MARTIN: *Una pistola!*

MOON: What a woman!

MARTIN: What a woman!

MOON: *Una pistola!*

GABRIELA: Behind every tree is a dark spirit,
a hungry one, and they watch me
through my bedroom window
and I want these spirits to know
I am armed and considered dangerous.

MARTIN: *(To the* MOON)
Something's wrong.
She ain't naked.
She's been naked every night
for two months, soon as the sun goes down,
walking back and forth, back and forth,
and you could see everything.

GABRIELA: I've taken measurements.
When we first moved here
each of these cactus trees
was twenty feet away.
Then one night I heard curious sounds.
I walked out here and thought I saw
the cactus trees moving toward the house.
I ran inside and got a tape measure—
and sure enough! Fifteen feet!
"Get over here, Benito," I shouted.
And Benito came and took measurements
and told me I was crazy
and went back to sleeping
and snoring and gyrating in the bed
and dreaming of Miss Panama
and Miss El Salvador
and Miss Teen Puerto Rico!
And I sit out here
and watch the cactus trees
inching closer and closer to my house
concealing dark and hungry spirits,
secret-keepers and heartbreakers.
Yesterday I measured the trees.
Ten feet! Ten feet exactly!
What's it going to take to make
Benito believe me?
Why does he think I make it up?

MARTIN: *(Frustrated)*
Ay, when is she gonna get naked?

GABRIELA: Am I alone, Moon?
Am I the only one who feels like this?

MOON: *(To* GABRIELA*)*
The people in this desert have their
own problems, *nena.*
In the house to your right
an insomniac is looking through
old photo albums.
Her eyes trace memories back
to their original moments:
a fifteenth birthday party,
a fight in a bar, a first kiss,
a young *novio* in uniform
who wanted babies right away.
She runs sleep-deprived fingers
over black and white photos,
trying to feel the skin
of that old *novio.*
But the paper yields nothing.
There are only secrets here.
The moment before the photo was taken
and the moment just after:
these moments are exiled
to those parts of the brain
reserved for all the forgotten things.
And this poor girl
re-enacts her nightly journey
toward understanding her past—
and every night,
inexplicably powerful currents
turn her away.

GABRIELA: Poor girl.

MOON: In the house to your left
an old man watches his old wife sleeping.
She breathes slowly
and he holds a mirror to her mouth.

A little cloud assures the old man
that she is alive.
He thinks of the day they first made love,
a sweet October day thousands of miles
and seasons from here.
He had never held a body
so rich with dreams
and she had never held a body
so hot, hairy and full of feral hunger,
and that first liquid night,
a night without food or sleep—
with my wicked light
coming in through their bedroom window—
as she lay in his exhausted arms...
he reached for a mirror
and put the mirror to her mouth
and she breathed on it—
proving to this young disbeliever
that she was indeed alive
and not a dream,
a woman and not a fabulous invention.
And now the old man is afraid
of life without her
and keeps a nine millimeter in his house
and he checks his wife's dutiful breathing
and knows what to do in case it ever stops.

GABRIELA: Poor old man.

CAT: (*To the* MOON)
Stop telling her those morbid stories
or she'll never rest!

GABRIELA: Poor girl, poor old man:
poor people everywhere.

(GABRIELA *starts to sob.*)

(*The* MOON *puts his violin down and comes down from the sky.*)

(As the MOON *gets closer to the ground, the* COYOTE *howls in pain.)*

COYOTE: OH GOD IT HURTS!
IT HURTS MY BODY SO MUCH!

CAT: Stop that hideous noise!

COYOTE: THE MOONLIGHT!
IT HURTS SO BAD!

*(*MARTIN *covers his ears.)*

MARTIN: That noise freakin' irritates.
Drives me crazy-insane!

(The COYOTE *howls even louder as the* MOON *gets closer to the backyard.)*

COYOTE: *(Struggling, in pain)*
The lunar light—
is sharp like daggers—
cuts into my skin—
ricochets off my nerves—
it's why coyotes howl
at the full moon!

(The MOON *enters the backyard.)*

(The COYOTE *passes out.)*

(The CAT *goes to the* COYOTE.*)*

CAT: Coyote? Coyote?

(The CAT *holds the* COYOTE.*)*

(The MOON *goes to* GABRIELA.*)*

MOON: There, there, Gabby.

GABRIELA: *(To the* MOON*)*
Oh, you didn't have to
come down here to—

MOON: But I wanted to.

CAT: *(Angry, to the* MOON*)*
Look what you did!

GABRIELA: Just an overly-sentimental
gun-toting Army housewife.

MOON: *(To* GABRIELA*)*
They say from the tears of women
are civilizations made.

GABRIELA: They really say that?

MOON: No, not really.

GABRIELA: Then why did you get my hopes up?

MOON: Shakespeare called me inconstant.

GABRIELA: I see why.

MOON: I never recovered from that.
The bastard!

CAT: Coyote? Speak to me!

(No response from the COYOTE*)*

(The CAT *cries.)*

GABRIELA: *(Laughs)*
Hey, Moon—
have you ever danced
with a woman holding a gun?

*(*GABRIELA *and the* MOON *dance.)*

MOON: From the tears of women
come mathematics sonatas
table manners the zipper
the *merengue* editorial pages
county fairs guitar strings
lipstick and the fables
of Jorge Luis Borges...

GABRIELA: You're trying to get into
my shorts, aren't you?

MOON: *(Faster, more excited)*
...brain surgery pickles
Macondo Mecca
the double play Bukowski tostones
and "Two Pieces of Bread
Expressing the Sentiment of Love."

GABRIELA: *(Gasps)*
Ay! References to Salvador Dali
make me hot!

(GABRIELA kisses the MOON passionately.)

(The CAT kisses the COYOTE passionately.)

CAT: *(To COYOTE)*
Those are very soft lips
you have for a wild animal.

GABRIELA: *(To MOON)*
Those are very soft lips
you have for a celestial object.

MARTIN: A strange transformation
is taking place in me
as I watch Gabriela
dance with the lucky moon.
I come here every night
to spy on a naked woman,
and hopefully see her thing.
But I'm bathed in the light of the moon
and as I listen to the words
of that gorgeous, spied-upon creature,
I'm changed completely.
The little boy who wanted
a cheap thrill is dead.
In his place, out of his cold remains,
rises a young man full of mature,
virile desire: a young man
in love with love!

(MARTIN *jumps down into the yard.*)

(GABRIELA *talks to the* MOON. *She and* MARTIN *speak in sync.*)

GABRIELA/MARTIN:
I [wanted/want] to touch [Benito's/her] skin
because I [wanted/want] to learn something.
Not about the temperature of [his/her] body.
Or how soft the hairs on [his/her] thing are.
Touching [his/her] skin [had/has] to do with...
testing the body's vibrations...
down past the glands and mute corpuscles...
down where bones talk
and the human body hums with music...
I [wanted/want] to find out
if we're tuned the same way.
What's the pitch of [his/her] soul?
Can I hear it if I tried?
Will I ever be able sing along with it?

MARTIN: *(To the* MOON*)*
I think she wants my ass.

GABRIELA: But Benito's little dick-brain
always interprets my touch
as nothing but a touch!
"Does this mean you wanna do it tonight?"
"No!" I'd say—
Jesus—he never understands...

MARTIN: A-ha!
She and the husband are incompatible!

GABRIELA: The idea of exploring
the notes and chords of each other's souls—
feels impossible now...

MOON: *(To* GABRIELA*)*
Yes, actually, I do, actually,

I, yes actually, yes, I do actually
want to get into your shorts.

MARTIN: *(To the* MOON*)*
Get in line you big stupid rock!

GABRIELA: I don't know what's happening in his mind.
The dreams of my husband are a mystery to me.
What secrets have abducted Benito from me?
Was it the war?

MOON: *(To* MARTIN*)*
I'll kick your ass, punk!

GABRIELA: What's funny is people always say,

if you want mystery, go to the moon.

MARTIN: He ain't mysterious.

MOON: You little—

MARTIN: He's been explored too much.
Too many little nasty footprints
and American flags on him!

MOON: I'll knock your block off—

GABRIELA: I say the deepest secrets
and the most confusing mysteries
aren't on the moon,
they're in the heart of the person
who lies next to you in bed every night.
Whole worlds go spinning around
their little orbits in there,
major civilizations
with their own alphabets
and food rituals
and ancient tales of love and woe
rise and fall in there—
and you can't get in there
to see for yourself.

MARTIN: I'll let you in,
mi vida, mi luz, mi alma!

(MARTIN *pushes the* MOON *away from* GABRIELA.)

GABRIELA: Who the hell are you?

MARTIN: Name's Martin.
Martin del Cuerpo Grande y Peludo.
And the moon can't love you like I can,
mi cielo, mi corazon, mi sangre,
mi extra-big sized box of Cocoa Puffs!

GABRIELA: What are you? Twelve?

MARTIN: Fourteen, *mi amor.*
And growing.
I have new hair
about to happen all over my body.

GABRIELA: I have a husband.
Seven-foot-six?
Two-eighty-five?

Owner of this and other firearms?
Coming home at seven A M?

MOON: (*To* MARTIN)
What do you mean I can't love her
like you can?

MARTIN: (*To the* MOON)
You're incontinent.
Shakespeare said.

MOON: "Inconstant" not "incontinent,"
you little fart!

(*The* MOON *and* MARTIN *fight.*)

(*The* MOON *takes the gun from* GABRIELA *and pistol-whips*
MARTIN. MARTIN *falls hard.*)

GABRIELA: *(To the* MOON*)*
Look what you did!
You're supposed to be romantic.

MOON: I did it for you.
How romantic can you get, *mujer*?

GABRIELA: *(To* MARTIN*)*
Kid. Hey kid.

MOON: *(To* GABRIELA*)*
Does this mean it's over—?

GABRIELA: *(To the* MOON*)*
Just get out of my face, all right?

*(*GABRIELA *tries to revive* MARTIN.*)*

(With a piece of chalk, the CAT *draws the outline of the dead* COYOTE *on the concrete.)*

(The dejected MOON *starts to go back into the sky.)*

MOON: I shouldn't get involved with people.
I should just watch.
That's what the moon does best.
Watches and bears witness—
then silently reports to you
through your dreams.
What are premonitions, hunches, déjà vu,
and the little voice in your head?
That's me—
whispering nightly in your ear,
hoping to give you a fighting chance
in this hard, carnivorous world.
Yes, Gabby, the trees are closing in on you.
Your visions of vampires and zombies are true.
And your husband's mind and heart
seem to have been kidnapped from you, poor girl.
So listen to the shadows, *nena*.

Pay attention to the lines between the lines.
That's the only way you're going

to survive out here,
at the edge of nowhere.

(The MOON *is back in the sky.)*

*(*GABRIELA *holds* MARTIN*.)*

GABRIELA: Poor Martin.
For you love is a mystery and a poem.
For me it's bad habits
and tricks that don't work any more.

MARTIN: *(Semi-conscious)*
...I'm gonna die an old man
who ain't never touched a woman's thing...

GABRIELA:
It's bones and hair and musky smells
and a lot of ambience that fades
with the daylight...

MARTIN: *(Semi-conscious)*
...when they bury virgins
they say that the grass
never grows on the grave...

GABRIELA: I have no way of knowing
what I'm going to do
when Benito comes home in the morning.
The house will seem too small.
He'll cry and shout in his sleep
as the truth fights to get out
while he dreams.
When I ask him about it,
he'll deny, deny, deny.

MARTIN: *(Semi-conscious)*
Sleep with me.

GABRIELA: The person I've chosen
left his body at the house
while his mind and soul travel
the solar system looking for love and laughs.

I wonder if I can get him back.
I wonder if I want him back.
I wonder if I care anymore.
I wonder if he cares where I've been.

MARTIN: *(Semi-conscious)*
I know you want babies.

GABRIELA: *(A sad laugh)*
I'll sleep with you.
But this is not
what you had in mind.

(GABRIELA lies on the ground next to MARTIN. They're not touching.)

MARTIN: *(Semi-conscious)*
Finally.
In the arms of a woman.

GABRIELA:
Tomorrow morning is going to bring changes.

MARTIN: *(Semi-conscious)*
It's better than I ever imagined.

GABRIELA: Big, great, awful changes.
I'm ready, Martin, are you?
I'm ready to make it happen—
and I'm ready for whatever happens to me.
Let it come.
Let the awful and beautiful changes come.

(GABRIELA and MARTIN fall asleep side by side.)

(The MOON plays the violin, something sad.)

(The COYOTE gets to his feet and walks away from the chalk outline of his dead body on the ground.)

(The CAT can't take her eyes off him.)

(The violin plays as the lights fade to black.)

END OF ACT ONE

.

ACT TWO

(Seven A M. GABRIELA's kitchen. Refrigerator, sink, stove, kitchen table and chairs.)

(BENITO, GABRIELA's husband, a Latino sergeant of 29, in full desert camouflage uniform and web gear, stands surrounded by duffel bags.)

(GABRIELA wears very tight cut-offs, tank top; she's shoeless.)

(She and BENITO haven't seen each other in two months.)

BENITO: Where were you?

GABRIELA: Backyard.

(BENITO and GABRIELA kiss briefly.)

BENITO: What's in the backyard?

GABRIELA: Slept there.

BENITO: Bed on fire?

GABRIELA: Just did, that's all.

BENITO: Huh. What's the coffee situation?

GABRIELA: As you wish, master.

BENITO: Call me master a lot, I really like it.

(GABRIELA makes coffee.)

GABRIELA: You lost a shitload of weight, soldier.

BENITO: God bless them M R Es.

GABRIELA: And nice circles under the eyes.

BENITO: Ain't slept in forty-eight.

GABRIELA: When are them fuckers gonna stop abusing my pretty, old man, huh?

BENITO: *(Looking at her hair)* Ain't no biggie, Gab.

GABRIELA: *(Re: her haircut)* You're looking at me like I'm...

BENITO: And you didn't mention the thing, the 'do, the nest...

GABRIELA: I was bored. You hate it.

BENITO: Ages you—but just a little—hardly nothing!—five or six years, max!

GABRIELA: *(Can't help but laugh)* Here's your stupid gun.

(GABRIELA hands BENITO his .9-millimeter pistol.)

BENITO: Not "gun", — "weapon". Your gun hangs between your legs.

GABRIELA: Nothing hangs between my legs, sergeant.

(BENITO eyes GABRIELA up and down with great male appreciation.)

BENITO: 'Cept me. Gabby. Oh, squeeze-able, eat-able, good-to-the-last-drop.

GABRIELA: I got a question. It's gonna sound, like stupid, but fucking laugh, I'll kick your ass back to Fort Irwin. Did you see the moon last night?

BENITO: *(Still on GABRIELA's body)* ...better than pogey-bait...

GABRIELA: Did you see the moon last night? I really gotta know this, Benito...

(GABRIELA looks at BENITO like his answer will decide everything.)

BENITO: The moon? Why on earth is a working man looking at the moon for?

GABRIELA: *(Disappointed)* 'Cause it was fucking huge, 'cause you once...

BENITO: The moon wearing a dress? Jerking itself off?

(GABRIELA *ignores him and opens the refrigerator.*)

GABRIELA: We're outta milk.

BENITO: *(Thinking about it)* Like maybe that's why they call it the Milky Way. The moon whacks off and comes all over the sky and *that's* how the Milky Way was born.

GABRIELA: Matter-of-fact, wise-ass, that ain't how it happened—

BENITO: No, no, please, not a lecture on...

GABRIELA: Fact is, the Milky Way was born outta, you know, little fluctuation thingies in space-time at the moment of the Big Bang.

BENITO: I like the way you say "Big" "Bang."

(GABRIELA *starts to leave.*)

GABRIELA: I'm going out, pick up some milk.

BENITO: Now?

GABRIELA: Cigarettes too, master?

BENITO: Stop calling me master, wench!

GABRIELA: Well, if you don't wanna come into the milk container and pour *that* in your cof—

BENITO: What is your God-given problem?

GABRIELA: *(Trying to leave)* Two minutes won't kill—

BENITO: But I just got back from the field!

GABRIELA:
Take a nap while I'm—

BENITO: And how come there's no milk?

GABRIELA: Okay, I'm going...

BENITO: What're you doing all day? It's the first. I'm back today. It's been today since like forever.

GABRIELA: I use milk. It runs out. I didn't go shopping. Why? I don't know.

BENITO: Too busy with the lesbian hair—?

GABRIELA: Too busy boning that cute Mexican boy lives next—

BENITO: That little fag?

GABRIELA: That "fag" helped me out while you were gone—

BENITO: *Coño*, girl, you are like...I don't know what...

GABRIELA: Yeah, well, welcome home.

BENITO: Feel welcomed too. It's been forever since I got kissed serious or groped around here—and the first thing you want is, you see my face, you're out the door! *(He goes to the refrigerator, opens it.)* There is nothing in here. It is a desert in here.

GABRIELA: Okay, Christ, I'm going...

BENITO: An empty fridge! That's like apocalyptic even! Ice cube trays full of sand. Not even a beer. *(He checks cabinets, drawers.)* Catfood, catfood, catfood. What? You mad at me or something? Mad at little old Benito for something he ain't got clue one what he done?

GABRIELA: Not exactly mad and learn *English*, please.

BENITO: "Not exactly mad?" Now that strikes terror. *Oye*. We're starting over. Re-starting the clock back. *(He exits and re-enters.)* Hi honey, I'm home! Back from the field. From two hundred cancer-making degrees. From boredom so perfect and rare it lacks a name. From nothing good to look at but the backsides of doorknobs with their thumb up their ass. Farm boys so interbred they can't tell a M16 from the gun between their legs.

GABRIELA: *(Can't help but laugh)* Why are soldiers such children?

BENITO: Better haul that face over here, *coño!*

(BENITO grabs GABRIELA and kisses her. This kiss evolves rapidly and they're all over each other. He tries to unzip her pants and take off his clothes during the following.)

GABRIELA: For a guy who ain't slept in forty-eight—

BENITO: *(Taking off his shirt)* Missed you like a sad broken son-of-a-bitch.

GABRIELA: *(Kissing him)* You taste so good, damn you, *Negro*...and I'm sorry I'm the dragon lady from hell, but I got—*Benito*—when I'm sleeping, I get these— what are you doing?

BENITO: *(Stripping fast)* Thought since you ain't seen a man in two months, you'd like to see what a man looks like.

GABRIELA: I got my period today.

BENITO: Hey, I'm liberal. Anyway, you think I'm afraid of a little blood?

GABRIELA: Like living with the author of the Song of Songs, I swear.

BENITO: *(Working her zipper)* You call Costco...?

GABRIELA: Just give me a minute to catch my breath...

BENITO: *(Working her zipper)* ...tell 'em you're out sick today...?

GABRIELA: Maybe let's get to know each other first?

BENITO: *(Working her zipper)* Why?

GABRIELA: Pull that zipper any lower and I'm yelling rape.

BENITO: *(Thinks it's a joke)* You're so funny.

GABRIELA: *Benito I'm fuckin' not fucking with you! (She pulls away, pulling up her zipper, shaking, fighting for control.)*

(BENITO looks at GABRIELA a cold, long moment.)

BENITO: I walked into some other dude's nightmare, *hija,* 'cause you ain't you. *(He collects his gear and starts to go offstage.)*

GABRIELA: You know the cat's missing?

(BENITO stops, turns to GABRIELA.)

BENITO: When I'm home from the field we leave words and other debris at the door, then close the motherfucking door.

GABRIELA: Did you hear what I said about the cat?

BENITO: Ain't the pussy I'm interested in right now...

GABRIELA: *Ay, Dios,* man, God, shit: go play with yourself!

BENITO: Is it my fault you got the Ass of Heaven?

GABRIELA: How many ways I gotta tell you I'm not some strip-artist whore-bitch you picked up in some German night club—?

BENITO: Then don't wear them shorts!

GABRIELA: Clawing at me like I'm a piece of twenty-five dollar street trash—

BENITO: You know where I can get it for twenty-five? Damn, point the way, girl!

GABRIELA: And it's hot. I wear shorts 'cause we live in Barstow and it's *July*?

BENITO: Okay, *nena,* that was a joke, I will not claw you, I will respect you, 'cause you are the farthest thing on earth from a twenty-five-dollar-German-whore-bitch-street-bitch-German-thing, really, I tell you the God's honest.

GABRIELA: You know you get crazy-insane when you're impatient?

BENITO: I'm human and male—so fuck me.

GABRIELA: You wanna hear about the cat or not?

BENITO: Bet half the company's in bed with their old ladies.

GABRIELA: Their old ladies are sex slaves and I'm not.

BENITO: *My* bad luck!

(GABRIELA *starts cleaning: washing dishes, wiping down counter tops, etc.*)

GABRIELA: I got home last night in a great mood. Had a great class. The kind that makes your mind go ballistic. You wanna know why?

BENITO: No, no, please don't tell me about your...

GABRIELA: We watch the night sky, what do we see? Billions of galaxies right? But *now* we think all those galaxies don't *really* exist...

BENITO: We do?

GABRIELA: 'Cause in space, light gets twisted...so looking at space is like looking through thousands of *mirrors* reflecting the same couple of galaxies over and over. Is that wild or what? The universe is an *optical illusion*. And it's lonelier than we ever thought.

BENITO: This kitchen's proof of that...

GABRIELA: So, I get home from school, mind fucking *bent* from all these thoughts, I call her, nothing. Then all night I'm hearing coyotes setting up camp under my window, whole *posses* of 'em, like, I don't know, like, like...

BENITO: *(Can't believe he's being ignored)* How come with you everything's gotta be "like" something else? Why can't shit just be what it is with you?

GABRIELA: *(Ignoring him)* ...like they opened up an asylum full of coyotes and they all parked their crazy asses in my backyard—howling like they're getting stabbed by the moonlight.

BENITO: Oh, that's clear, thank you.

GABRIELA: I think they ate my cat. One you gave me for my birthday?

BENITO: Maybe *I'll* get that milk—

GABRIELA: The cat's devoured. Mind's all like—
Christ: *no!* —thinking of her maimed to death by wild animals chewing her flesh. And I think it's gotta mean something, Benito. Like the Buddha says: there's no coincidences.

BENITO: The Buddha?

GABRIELA: I decided I let too much of life walk past me unwatched. That life is fulla signals that teach you shit. And I've been blind like I didn't wanna know. So I'm thinking that something like this doesn't happen for no reason, the cat, and I'm pondering what those reasons might be and asking myself: what other signs of important things have I been missing lately? You know. About us. And shit that's going on.

BENITO: *(Making a shopping list)* Beer, milk, bullshit remover, strap-ons—oops, cut the—

GABRIELA: This desert...that's the thing...it's like, like...

BENITO: Wait, I'll do it. It's like...a nuclear beast ate up the whole world with all its flaming teeth, and left nothing for us but the deep-fried leftovers in the Tupperware of Human Shit.

GABRIELA: Not even close. I mean, *coño*, Benito, I'm a tropical woman, I'm not used to this shit.

BENITO: Grand Concourse ain't tropical.

GABRIELA: And with you in the field, and the cat missing, it's lonely as *fuck* here.

BENITO: Loneliness is your choice, *nena*.

GABRIELA: No one sane chooses this.

BENITO: If you didn't look down on all my buds and their wives who tried hard to make friends with you and found it *impossible*.

GABRIELA: Those Barbie Dolls your buddies are saddled with? Those wooden pieces of perpetual blow-job machines—?

BENITO: This language is offensive. Period.

GABRIELA: I tried making friends. But it's a scientific fact: the brain can only gossip 'bout soap operas for so long before it starts to puke on itself. Or maybe I just got tired spending my afternoons with those girls, with cucumbers in our mouths, practicing blow-jobs.

BENITO: You were getting a valuable lesson!

GABRIELA: *Coño*, like I need one! Benito ... how do I say this, how do I...? Benito...you don't know the desert like a civilian does. Like I do. The desert is quiet. Nothing in it moves. It looks almost gentle. So you think, damn, if nothing in it moves, maybe it's safe for you. You can go take a walk in it. You can lie on the ground and stare at the moon.

BENITO: Ay, this moon crap again. All the moon is is future landfill, Gab.

GABRIELA: Shakespeare didn't think so. He called it inconstant.

BENITO: And I care!

GABRIELA: It has its ways, the desert, that it knows how to ... consume you. So many ways to get you tricked. So you trust it. Stupid you: you go out in the desert and coyotes jump your ass and eat you. The sun bakes you. The night-cold freezes blood. The bigness of it scares your heart and makes it stop. Okay—so then you *don't* go outside. You're stuck inside—over at the friggin' Costco or the commissary on post or a sorry-ass movie in Victorville with the Barbie Dolls. But then everyone you see in the dark air conditioning's like ... vampires sizing you up for the next dinner. Strangers make you feel small and stupid. Couples with their fancy fingers all inside each other's pants remind you your old man's not around. On the movie screen is life all full of big blood and sex and people making perfect funny jokes every time. Like to remind you nobody really laughs in your world when you're alone. And that's what my life has been like, Benito, okay? And you know what? It really sucks! It's really a shitty thing to do to a person!

BENITO: So what are you telling me? Tell me what you're telling me and stop telling me the other shit you're not telling me.

GABRIELA: They stick you in a war. I don't see you for a year. I finally get you home *moments,* it feels like, not enough time to take your temperature, get used to your smell or know why you cry in your sleep—boom! —we're shipped to the desert and you're off to the field again!

BENITO: This is my job we're talking about, right? What are you saying about my job?

GABRIELA: I'm saying fuck your job, okay?

BENITO: That's telling me something. I'm telling you: not to worry about the desert, in a year it's Germany.

GABRIELA: Oh, that's a step up. That's the highway to self-respect.

BENITO: Well, what am I supposed to do?! Will you tell me that?! Dammit to fucking hell on *earth*, Gabriela!

GABRIELA: Don't yell at—

BENITO: I am in the—what? Let's read aloud the little tag here on my...sez—ARMY! I am in the Army. In the Army you travel. That's what the Army is, homegirl! A great motherfucker of a travel agency. And they don't recommend all nice and sweat-free: *they order you!* One year it's Germany where the whole country is full of Germans, and I'm sorry but we tried to get rid of the Germans, but dammit, the Germans didn't want to go! Then the next year it's the desert. Oh, the desert's hot! It's boring! Full o' vermin! The Army wives never finished pre-school. I hate the blow-job lessons! But in case you didn't notice, your car runs on oil and there's this place where oil comes from and everybody wants a piece of that sucker but if you want anything on God's goofy earth you gotta display the size of your *cojones*, and oh my God, the Middle East is in a desert!

GABRIELA: I know where the damn—

BENITO: *(On a roll)* We train soldiers in the art of desert warfare—where? —in the desert! *Ay Dios mio!* I go out to the field for months at a time—why? —'cause they pay my ass! I don't like it. I don't want it. But I didn't feel like cutting pineapple the rest of my life in some Puerto Rican Plantation of Death. I told you I'm staying in the Army twenty years and retiring at the ripe old age of thirty-eight, pocket a full pension and never for a second sweat the money shit for as long as I have life, never. Told you that our first date, running out of that bar with skinheads chasing us. I got nine years left on the meter, Gabby. More than half the way there. So the next nine years, *nena*, is Germany or the

desert, Germany or the desert, snow or sand, Nazis or
knuckleheads, back and forth like that assuming war
don't break out and I'm not protecting goat-herders
in Somalia! That's the trip you signed on to take. Are
there any questions, Private?

GABRIELA: No sir, master, sir. *(She pours all the coffee she
just made down the sink.)*

BENITO: You gotta stop acting like you know more than
everybody.

GABRIELA: I do know more than everybody.

BENITO: Then keep it to yourself, 'cause, like the
Buddha says, it's a turn off.

GABRIELA: *(Laughs)* Oh, *that's* funny!

BENITO: Everything you say and do reflects on me—

GABRIELA: Turn off? I'm the one that's off.

BENITO: You get into a car accident, it's my rates that go
up. You break the law, it's my rank that's busted—

GABRIELA: My eyes, my senses—*off.* My ideas—*off.*
My—oh fuck it—now we're just going in circles here.
Talking in and out of the same three sentences—as if,
like, more words means more communicating. Ain't
that a joke? Let me get that milk. *(She goes for her car
keys.)*

BENITO: You got no clue of my life's insanity out
there— 'cause I make this army shit look easy. Look
graceful. That's why you don't know jack how fucked
it is for me.

GABRIELA: What're you bitching about?

BENITO: The last month in the field, for me, I got my
ass stuck in Star Wars, Gabby, okay? That's where I
was. *Inside.* Behind a *desk.* In front of a *computer screen.*
I went outta my mind. I'm going to the Captain, going,
Sir, I wanna be outside. If I'm gonna play G I Joe I

wanna be in an M1A1 or jumping out of a chopper or blowing expensive stuff up, not in a goddamn *building* with *air* conditioning. But no. Captain rules. So I'm in Star Wars now.

GABRIELA: Why don't you give me one good clue—?

BENITO: It's like this. The desert floor is covered big time with sensors connected to satellites tracking every piece of moving hardware we got out there—Abrams, Cobras, A P Cs—our side and the bad guys. So the grunts and gun bunnies go through their combat simulations, right?, and on a computer in this building called Star Wars what happens in the field is monitored in real time. So I gotta watch this computer screen and see how the battles go. That's what I did for weeks of my life I'll never get back.

GABRIELA: That's cause for bitching? You're sitting in air conditioning! It's the Mojave!

BENITO: Gabriela, I don't wanna sit. Sitting is for *officers.* For *points.* A man does not sit when he *works.*

GABRIELA: Yeah, but, think—you could—maybe there's training here you can pick up, you know, learn a, you know—

BENITO: Skill? That I can use in the "real world"?

GABRIELA: It saves on your body, you don't gotta wreck yourself...

BENITO: Just waste away like some puke college professor—

GABRIELA: I just don't think you should be like some common foot soldier—

BENITO: I am no common anything, okay?

GABRIELA: I just think this shows the Captain—

BENITO: What? Wants to get his prep school lips around my joint? He pulled me out of a line of men. This has nothing to do with me at all.

GABRIELA: So what are you afraid of?

BENITO: Go shoot yourself.

GABRIELA: No, I'm asking you something—

BENITO: No, no, no, no, I know how the mind is working now, it's so obvious, Gabby, c'mon. "Benito hates to use his brain. Benito don't know a good thing when it's staring straight into his baboon face!" You know what I turned into out there? A man watching other men work. Then I had to write a "narrative description" of all the things the men did while they worked. So I'm in front of a half-billion dollars of pure high tech and with two little chopstick fingers I take a half hour to type out three sentences and I can't spell half the words I have to write. That's my job.

GABRIELA: But nobody shot at you, did they?

(BENITO *throws his arms in the air and sits at a kitchen chair, facing downstage, his back to* GABRIELA.)

BENITO: What did I do? What did I do? Huh? I just want you to take your top off!

GABRIELA: *(Sarcastic)* Stop, you're getting me so horny.

BENITO: Damn, I'm, like, out there, in no man's land, pretending to have war except all the hardware is more real than me, but the conflict is a game, it's fiction, and that's my job, and I come home to you, all beautiful, like what you see after death and the angels greet you in the morning, and you hope, you know, God allows sex with the angels in Heaven maybe once in a while if you're extra good around Christmas, but everything between us is real war, honey, and it's getting old real fast, baby, I'm telling you.

(BENITO *closes his eyes and they stay closed during the following.*)

GABRIELA: Tell you what I don't get, *Negro*. How, like, a feeling, which is made of nothing, can burn a hole in your stomach...or make a lump in your throat heavy as a man. A lump you wake up with...and stays with you until you go to bed...

BENITO: *(Eyes closed)* Enough. I just got back from the field. You don't know me. I don't know you. It's your usual freak-out, when I come home.

GABRIELA: But it's the first time you were in the field since the war and I'm like all outta practice being your wife...

BENITO: *(Eyes closed, sleepy)* ...we'll get over it, like we always...

GABRIELA: ...and I'm having dreams every single night and all of them want me to test you...

BENITO: *(About to fall asleep)* Stop. Just stop with that. Don't tell me no more about dreams...

(Silence from GABRIELA *for a second.)*

(BENITO falls asleep in the chair.)

(GABRIELA takes off his boots.)

GABRIELA: Jesus, I forget how much space you take up. And you got that tank smell. Soon you'll be leaving pubes on the tile. And, like, if I think things now—am I gonna know which thoughts are mine 'cause they're mine or they're mine 'cause you put them there...

(MARTIN enters holding a large cardboard box.)

MARTIN: Where's my reward, woman?

(GABRIELA sees her cat inside the box.)

GABRIELA: I was ready to call the fucking morgues for you, cat!

MARTIN: Found her surrounded by coyotes all salivating and doing the humpy motion with their torsos. She was next to a cat skeleton. We think it's the remains of Pinky Garcia.

GABRIELA: *(To cat)* Better not catch no rabies, you!

MARTIN: Looks like she got some animal-on-animal last night.

GABRIELA: Good thing you're fixed. I don't feel like raising a bunch of mutant coyote-cats.

MARTIN: *(Re* BENITO*)* No one's worried about the noise level?

GABRIELA: He'll sleep for seven straight, I swear, *days.* *(She puts the cat in another room.)*

MARTIN: I'm going to the store, you want anything?

*(*GABRIELA *gives* MARTIN *money.)*

GABRIELA: Ten for the cat rescue: now go.

MARTIN: You saying you don't want me around no more?

GABRIELA: I'm saying my old man's back from the field and has a limited sense of humor when it comes to who he thinks wants to fuck me.

MARTIN: Wow, that sounds so sexual.

GABRIELA: How do you even know concepts of the human body?

MARTIN: I'm only saying I know you want babies. I'm old enough to get you pregnant.

GABRIELA: Just hope your dick's not a small as your brain!

MARTIN: That's so mean!

GABRIELA: Look, fine, we had some fun, playing touch football, whatever, but recess time is over, the bell rang junior, time to get on the school bus and go home.

MARTIN: I'm growing pecs.

GABRIELA: My man is back and he's got rules and regulations.

MARTIN: I wouldn't ask you to serve me. I can wash my own *ropa*. I would bring you hot *huevos* in the morning. Read the *periodico* to you. Put your *pelo* up in bobby pins. Keep your *piso* waxed. Your *cocina* full of canned creamy soup and Cocoa Puffs. Okay, *nena*?

GABRIELA: Out, please.

MARTIN: I don't need to be big and strong. I can handle your nightmares if you tell them to me. I love a house full of singing and fresh desert air. I'll even tolerate your cat. Don't answer right away, Gabby. But think about it.

GABRIELA: You're fourteen.

MARTIN: Can I see it?

GABRIELA: No.

(GABRIELA *starts pushing* MARTIN *out the door.*)

MARTIN: I saw you sleeping in the backyard again. I know this isn't paradise, Gabby. Hey—wasn't that a great fucking moon last night?

(MARTIN *gives* GABRIELA *a kiss on the cheek and goes.*)

(GABRIELA *looks at* BENITO *a long moment, watching him sleep. She comes downstage of him and sits cross-legged on the floor, facing upstage. She takes off her top, exposing herself to* BENITO, *who continues to sleep.*)

BENITO: *(Sleeping)* Gabby's having dreams...

(*It seems to become night in the kitchen. The* CAT *and the* COYOTE *appear, watching.*)

GABRIELA: ...her dreams are full of broken moonlight, Benito...her dreams are full of moist sex and the dirty smells of sweat and desire...her dreams level civilizations and make them grateful for chaos and heavy breathing and whirlwinds...

BENITO: ...Gabby's having awful dreams...

(GABRIELA *holds herself and tries hard to keep from crying and* BENITO *sleeps and the lights go to black.*)

END OF ACT TWO

(*Intermission*)

ACT THREE

(That night)

(GABRIELA's bedroom. On the walls: photos of tanks, BENITO's military citations, a poster of Salvador Dali's Two Pieces of Bread Expressing the Sentiment of Love, *a black velvet unicorn poster. Military swords are displayed over the headboard. A stack of books and a telescope next to the bed.)*

(The light of the MOON comes in through upstage windows.)

(There are occasional maddening offstage howls of coyotes.)

(BENITO lies in bed, fast asleep, bootless and minus the web gear, but otherwise dressed as he was at the end of ACT TWO.)

(GABRIELA lies at his side, dressed in sweatshirt and sweatpants. She holds a mirror to BENITO's mouth, watching his breath clouding the glass, leaning close to him.)

(BENITO cries in his sleep. He sounds like a wounded coyote. He thrashes. Alarmed, GABRIELA shakes him awake.)

(BENITO wakes with a gasp. Without looking or thinking he takes a swing at GABRIELA.)

(GABRIELA instinctively pulls back and BENITO misses. He's disoriented, breathing hard.)

BENITO: *Never*...never wake me up like that, *nena,* if you don't want your teeth on the floor.

GABRIELA: *(Shaken)* I'm sorry. I forgot. It's been a while, remember?

BENITO: Shit; shit; that whacked my nerves up pretty bad. It's the same day?

GABRIELA: I'm not sure what's the day.

BENITO: You okay? I didn't—?

GABRIELA: Some instinct in me remembered you've been doing that since the war.

BENITO: Everything's swirling in this room, *carajo.* Must be all the drugs I don't take but wish I did...

(Groaning, BENITO *unsteadily gets out of bed and goes to the offstage bathroom.)*

*(*GABRIELA *talks to the offstage* BENITO *as he takes a leak.)*

GABRIELA: You were talking in your dreams.

BENITO: *(Offstage)* I never dream.

GABRIELA: Everyone does. It's only human.

BENITO: *(Offstage)* I ain't only human. I'm human-plus.

GABRIELA: I heard you making noises. Like something was coming outta someplace in you, someplace down and low, like where your bones talk.

BENITO: *(Offstage)* This just in: bones don't talk.

GABRIELA: *If* they did. You cry in your sleep too. So quiet maybe only a bat could hear it. So secret, too, the air that brings it up from inside you hardly makes a scratch in the mirror I held all day long to your mouth, 'cause I was afraid you were dead sometimes.

BENITO: *(Offstage)* I'm so glad to know that.

GABRIELA: *(More to herself)* It's kinda screwed up: of all the parts of the body, only the brain gets the power to speak. I'd love to know what your stomach thinks.

*(*BENITO *comes in from the bathroom.)*

BENITO: My stomach thinks you're mental. Other organs have their own viewpoints on this.

(During the following, BENITO *strips down to his boxers—a not-so-subtle striptease for* GABRIELA.*)*

GABRIELA: *(Amused by him)* ...Okay, here's what I don't get. How come in eleven years in the Army I never heard you or any of your pinhead friends say one honest patriotic thing?

BENITO: *(Stripping)* I love my country. It's the people in it I hate.

GABRIELA: Makes me laugh to think of you risking your life for a bunch of tree huggers.

BENITO: *(Stripping)* Immigrants, welfare queens...

GABRIELA: Welfare? C'mon! What was the house in Germany we didn't pay for? That pumped-up car? That ain't taxpayer money being wasted?

BENITO: Taxpayer's getting a lean, mean fighting machine—with a nice ass.

GABRIELA: Who can't stop crying in his sleep like an infant baby.

*(*BENITO *gets into bed.)*

BENITO: Every soldier does that. It's nothing. Justifies the combat pay.

GABRIELA: If it's nothing what's the big crime in telling me?

BENITO: ...And how come there's sand in here? And what's with the ugly pajamas?

GABRIELA: You think, oh your mind's this distant private place, what happens in there only happens to you—but it happens to me, too—

BENITO: It's gotta lighten up in here or I'll mistake this bed for the bottom of Death Valley.

GABRIELA: I tell you every passing thing that hits my mind, Benito.

BENITO: *(Sarcastic)* And it ain't as boring as scrubbing a barracks floor with a Q-tip.

(GABRIELA looks at BENITO a silent moment.)

GABRIELA: Oh. It's my job to entertain you, huh? And if I don't do my job, I might as well do something else tonight. *(She gets out of bed and starts changing her clothes.)*

BENITO: What are you doing?

GABRIELA: If I hurry, I can catch the second half of my class.

BENITO: Tonight? You're going to school—?

GABRIELA: It's been tonight since about forever.

BENITO: You always quit your classes when I'm home from the field. That's been the deal—

GABRIELA: But this one, we spend hours looking up—and I never do that in real life. It makes me aware of the fucking universe, okay?

BENITO: Gabby, for crying out loud—

GABRIELA: *Exactly* what you been doing all day in your sleep. Driving me crazy with the sound of pain that's busting your gut. Making me wonder what's in there, thinking the worst, holding my breath for an answer, getting *zero*. You want me to stay? Give me a husband that's more than a body in my bed, okay?

BENITO: *Oyeme, nena, por Dios*, it was ... nothing. A thing. I did a thing, after the ground war I never told you about. Messed my head a little. Now get back in—

GABRIELA: *(Getting her telescope)* School's twenty minutes away, I'll be back in—

BENITO: Maybe *you* get something outta pulling barbed wire out of a person, but the person *doing* it *suffers*. Humans like to put pain to *rest*.

GABRIELA: Silence never rests nothing.

BENITO: The *balls* you have!

GABRIELA: You expect me to lie in bed and spread my legs—for who? A stranger? Benito—hello—who are you?

BENITO: One tired son-of-a-bitch is who.

GABRIELA: I promised to God that whatever they throw at you, I'd help you take care of it, if you let me, if I know how. But I can't do it if I don't know what happened.

BENITO: You're not gonna like it, Gab.

GABRIELA: I'm not promising to like it, I'm not promising not to be mad, I'm promising to listen.

(Beat)

BENITO: Okay, the war was over. We were pacifying little towns left and right. So small you're afraid the wind will blow them away. So the ragheads had these big time curfews—like if three or more hang out on a street corner, boom, automatic arrest, no questions asked, off to Saudi and them in their monkey-language all pissed off at you. So the scene's all pacified and I'm just hangin' with a couple of treadheads contemplating playing spades on the downtime, it's *that* mellow—when—some idiot—fires a rocket at the A P C I'm standing next to and blows a hole in it the size of Kuwait and decimates one of my corporals. And I'm telling you, I'm tripping. I'm like insane over this event. I'm stomping around the desert like baby Godzilla, cursing the little Persian freaks and I got wild, Gabby, you know what I did? The war is over and you know what I did? I called for fire. I'm the F. O.

out there and I get on the horn and I call an air strike
and I leveled a town. Precision-guided munitions
fell by the ton on a little town 'til every shack, every
Mosque and shithouse where people lived their
tortured camelshit lives got turned to dust and wind
'cause of me. After the bombs stopped falling a place
that used to be on a map got de-mapped from earth
and that happened 'cause they pissed off an American
soldier. They pissed off the man in your bed.

(GABRIELA *looks at* BENITO, *then goes to him.*)

GABRIELA: Oh, my baby...I'm so sorry...

(GABRIELA *kisses* BENITO.)

BENITO: Gabby...

GABRIELA: ...just think it's better ... you let this out of
you ... you won't be hunted in your sleep by the death
of your friend no more...

(BENITO *looks at* GABRIELA.)

BENITO: What death?

GABRIELA: Your corporal. You must've lost your shit
when he died. No wonder you—

BENITO: Uhm—he didn't *die*, Gabby.

GABRIELA: He didn't? What do you mean he—?

BENITO: Got *wounded* is what.

GABRIELA: Like—fatal-wounded? Lots of blood?

BENITO: His hand.

GABRIELA: Got blown off?

BENITO: Motherfuckers blew off his fingers!

GABRIELA: Wait a minute. A village in Iraq for a—?

BENITO: Very important fingers!

GABRIELA: You leveled it 'cause one of your buddies
got a *pinky* wound?

BENITO: We evacuated them *first*, Gabby.

GABRIELA: You let them out before the bombs fell?

BENITO: *Most* of them anyway.

GABRIELA: Some people stayed and died?

BENITO: Ones that didn't *listen*—

GABRIELA: Women and children—?

BENITO: I can't control what happens in the mind of a raghead. Did they go? Some did. Others not. In a war...

GABRIELA: Which was over, you said.

BENITO: In a rural pacification program...

GABRIELA: I hate your job. I really do. That's all I'm saying here.

BENITO: Swear, *nena*, you are unlimited in your ballbusting gifts! I'm trained to respond: what could I do?

GABRIELA: Not call the air strike?

BENITO: You weren't there. You don't know. We didn't know. We were in a *situation*, Gabby, blood, tension, enemies, heat, howling pain, adrenaline surge could give the Vatican a hard-on...

GABRIELA: You never do shit like that.

BENITO: It bothers you, we'll call an Army shrink.

GABRIELA: Is it crazy if I don't like to think of you as a cold-blooded killer? If I don't like when they take my husband and make him kill like this?

BENITO: *Way* outta line, Private—

GABRIELA: You hate it too! You do! *Inside* you do! If you didn't, you wouldn't cry every time you close your eyes—

BENITO: I do this thing—you're right, I hold it in— 'cause I'm afraid to disturb you—okay, *este*—we got off on the wrong foot this morning, let's communicate—let me give you every growling demon inside me making all the noise that keeps me up at night, and I say, girl kill this fucker for me, 'cause I can't, bury this creature 'cause it's torturing me, and you go and put on fangs and torture me some more.

GABRIELA: You don't sound tortured. You sound proud you erased a town and wrote your name in its dust—but I don't believe it. I think it's a lie you tell yourself so you can survive the Army.

BENITO: Sure about that? Maybe I liked watching the bombs fall.

GABRIELA: Don't say that, you didn't like it, Benito.

BENITO: Fine! I'm boycotting telling you anything serious anymore! (*He gets out of bed.*)

GABRIELA: That's cool 'cause you know what I did when you went to war I boycotted telling you about?

BENITO: You had an affair with an Iraqi.

GABRIELA: I had an affair with a guy named Muhammad.

BENITO: That better be an allegory of speech.

GABRIELA: I took a class in Bamholder on Arabs. I read about Islam. I didn't know jack about those people, but I thought—

BENITO: Hey. How do you clear an Iraqi bingo room? Yell B-52.

GABRIELA: I thought: he's going out to kill them, then I wanna know who they are—

BENITO: Why do Iraqi men have mustaches? So they can look like their mothers.

GABRIELA: —I learned about this orphan Muhammad, who believed in Jesus and humility and created a kneeling prayer 'cause his people were too proud to kneel to their God and he thought that was bullshit. An angel grabbed him by the nuts and said: "recite!" And he recited and didn't stop for twenty years and practically invented his people's language when he did.

BENITO: I'm getting your library card burned on national television and the country will cheer.

GABRIELA: I thought—if I learned something about those people you're dropping "precision-guided munitions" on, I could respect them, and my respect, maybe, would balance out what you were doing, in a Karma way.

BENITO: A Karma way. Giving aid and comfort to the enemy—

GABRIELA: Nobody got any aid or comfort as I thought of you risking your ass for nothing.

BENITO: Freedom ain't nothing! Freedom ain't nothing! Freedom ain't nothing!

GABRIELA: How do you bomb a town to make it free?

BENITO: I married a fucking hippie! It's *over*, Gabriela. Good guys won. Good guys come home. Good guys pick up where they left off.

GABRIELA: It's never over. Spoken or not, a soldier takes his battles with him everywhere he goes. You taught me that.

BENITO: Not tonight: no. Tonight we're exempted from all shit. Tonight nothing gets through to us.

(BENITO *gets back into bed and kisses* GABRIELA.)

GABRIELA: Benny, I'm not trying to bust your balls...I just wish I had the words...for all the *thinking* I've been...

BENITO: At the edge of the bed, the soldier is just a man again. *(Before she can stop him, he pulls her closer.)* Tonight we're taking inventory. Reading all the pages on this fine book of photographs. Maybe we'll remember why we're here. What's this?

(BENITO points to the scar on GABRIELA's knee. It's an old game of theirs.)

GABRIELA: That was the morning I fell off the roof of my house playing Super Puerto Rican Girl with *Boriqua* Power and I caught the corner of a fridge we kept outside, with my knee.

BENITO: A beautiful jagged mess. Like your mind. This?

(BENITO kisses GABRIELA's scar and points to her thigh.)

GABRIELA: That was the afternoon my brother thought it'd be radically cute to plunge a fish hook bone-deep in my thigh. Repeatedly.

BENITO: Remind me to remove his entire thorax. This?

(BENITO kisses GABRIELA's scar and touches her arm.)

GABRIELA: The night *Abuela* thought it'd be a howling pisser to stick the burning butt-end of a Marlboro here and see how high I'd jump.

BENITO: Serious need for a lobotomy, that bearded old bitch, for hurting you in any way, shape, or form. That's my real job. To hurt what hurts you. *(Sees a scar he's never seen before.)* What's this?

GABRIELA: Oh. Mexican kid next door asked me to played touch football and I slipped and cut myself.

BENITO: He changed your body! Who said your body's supposed to change, huh?

(BENITO starts to kiss GABRIELA.)

GABRIELA: Poor Benito's old lady keeps changing on him...can't even remember to keep a cold beer in the house...a pain in his very nice ass. Why do you put up with it, *Negro*?

(GABRIELA *kisses him deep. Surprised, not daring to hope for too much,* BENITO *kisses her again.*)

(*She responds quickly—covering him in hungry kisses, her arms and legs around and around him.*)

(*They make love. It's fast and raw.*)

(*Silence*)

(*She lies on her back, staring at the ceiling.*)

(*He lies next to her, eyes closed.*)

(*Then she pulls away.*)

(*She quietly starts to cry. She doesn't want him to hear, so she tries to cover it, but he hears and reaches for her.*)

(*She quickly gets out of bed. She puts on jeans T-shirt and shoes.*)

(*He watches her, motionless.*)

BENITO: You still going to that class?

GABRIELA: (*Shaking her head no*) I'm leaving. You.

BENITO: You're leaving. Me.

(GABRIELA *packs clothes.*)

GABRIELA: I have some money from Costco I saved up, I'll take the little car, I'll live in Victorville, or Los Angeles, or Vegas, I don't really know at this...

BENITO: You only think you're leaving me.

GABRIELA: I ain't slept in that bed since you left for the field—

BENITO: Come back in the bed, please.

GABRIELA: —for two months I slept in the backyard— naked, sometimes—half-hoping those coyotes'd eat me.

(BENITO *gets out of bed and grabs* GABRIELA *roughly.*)

BENITO: The fuck you're leaving! Let's see you leave if I don't let you.

GABRIELA: *(Pushing back)* Don't push me, okay? I'll kick your ass!

BENITO: You're gonna kick my ass?

GABRIELA: Kick it all the way to Baghdad!

BENITO: You got somebody else? Little La Raza boy-toy next door?

GABRIELA: Please. Do I look that stupid to you?

BENITO: Friggin' great news, Gab!

GABRIELA: I thought—I'm so stupid and this proves it—I thought: no, I can't leave while you're in the field—you come home to an empty house—so out of *fairness*, a sense of *justice*, I'll make you see I'm drowning in the sand and the cold ---

BENITO: Swear you use words like some people use razor wire and guard dogs.

GABRIELA: And maybe you'd see it, clearly, finally—

BENITO: When did you put on all these clothes I never seen before?

GABRIELA: —and you'd decide, for me, for my fucking life, *leave* the Army, turn your back on this deadly shit—

BENITO: It's so unfair! When I go to the field, I need for you not to *change*!

GABRIELA: —I could finally, finally see what it's like to be married to you in a different way—

BENITO: One crudely stupid selfish woman—

GABRIELA: Not in an Army town, where everybody's armed like the end of the world. Not smelling like tank fuel. Not playing God. Not one of us living a life the other can't understand anymore. But it's never gonna happen is it—?

BENITO: No—there's no—there's no—no—no—no!

GABRIELA: No—'cause—the Army's got you by the balls. And you like it! I'll tell you something—I'll share many things—I do share many things—but I won't share your balls! Not any more!

BENITO: One total messed-up mental case...

GABRIELA: And who wouldn't get like that? The Ass of Heaven's got no real education 'cept what she scrapes together from night schools. Got no life-long friends. Got no experience but friggin' temp work 'cause of all our moving. I'd like to actually maybe be something someday better than working at Costco all my life. I'd like to make more than minimum wage before I'm thirty-eight. If you could just—listen—walk away from this life, *mi cielo*, and I know that would be so hard for you...

BENITO: You can't decide shit like this in secret.

GABRIELA: But if you quit the Army...imagine for me, *Negro*: living where people wear clothes instead of uniforms, and nobody salutes nobody...

BENITO: This some kind of gruesome test?

GABRIELA: ...and maybe we can both go back to school...

BENITO: Me and school? Are you cracked? I read at a fourth grade level, you wanna know the absolute.

GABRIELA: I'll teach you to read better. I can do that. It don't kill your manhood to learn something from your wife, Benito. *Coño*, man, I grew up thinking I was stupid, but now I know on Neptune, it rains diamonds...

BENITO: You're leaving 'cause I don't read books enough? Don't know about Buddha and Allah and Salvador Dali?

GABRIELA: *(Won't take the bait)* I tried so hard to love what you love, see the purpose in it, to hate your enemies, I mean really hate them. But I can't fake it anymore...now, maybe, if you could love what I love...

BENITO: You think I'm common, but I'm not. I jump out of planes. I climb mountains. I swim the ocean. I know martial arts. I can survive in the middle of nowhere with nothing but shoe string and a mirror. I can take apart an M16A2 and put it back together blindfolded. I speak three languages. I met the Secretary of Defense. I defended an oppressed country against naked *aggression.* I was in history. Is none of that any good anymore?

GABRIELA: Of course it is—but it cost one of us a whole life. I followed you all over the earth. Lived in lonely little towns where I never knew the language. Where old German ladies looked at me like I dropped napalm on their babies. And the cold there...cold like when you're abandoned by God. Cold like the fingers of a baby's corpse. Cold that fucks you and gives you a virus. Oh, and then nobody in the South can tell if I'm black or white!

BENITO: And you didn't get nothing back? You had parents wanted to haul your ass to Alcatraz. You had intimate knowledge of the juvenile *penal* system when we met.

GABRIELA: When we met—yeah—your uniform had stars on it. Yeah, you were my warrior who looked at the sky and pretended there were faces of loved ones on the moon. But then, the stars on you started to fade. God, why didn't I say something years ago?

BENITO: A house, a car, protection from the sun,
lots of eats, love, you get love, because I stupidly,
ridiculously, fanatically love you—you get that? —you
see that in the plus column? Should I repeat? It's the
love, stupid!

GABRIELA: Please don't throw that word around like a
fucking hand grenade...

BENITO: I'm sorry I love you *and* the Army. I'm
sorry I have two loves. But one, you might notice, is
inanimate. Ain't got a soul. Can't really compete.

GABRIELA: It's doing not-so-bad, I think!

BENITO: What you really want is for me to like literally
attach myself surgically to the hip. Well, here's the big
Geraldo newsflash, *nena*: one hundred percent of me?
Not available in any store. Why? 'Cause I need to be—
don't even think of laughing—someplace, whatever,
that's my privacy: where you can't go.

GABRIELA: This just in: I know.

BENITO: I get that private thing in the field sometimes.
When I'm out there, I sometimes can feel—all the
previous wars. Feel them in my body. My chest. No
wonder that's where they put the medals. Out there
training, before they stuck my ass in Star Wars, I tried
to even feel, you know, Korea in me, even Vietnam.
Men doing impossible things together. Men agreeing.

GABRIELA: Men, men, men...

BENITO: With codes and rules on how to be. Instead of
all the chaos puked on the world by eunuchs with no
codes and no rules—all pussywhipped, worried about
exchange rates, big weekend warriors, playing their
mindgames on the weak: just sliding from moment
to moment like there was no absolutes for valor and
manhood and freedom.

GABRIELA: You joined the Army 'cause you were poor.

BENITO: And I ain't poor no more. And I don't mean the Grand National parked outside. I mean in me, my mind: the war on poverty ended and I won it.

GABRIELA: Who's prouder of you than me? I just think—you're only using a tenth or a millionth of this great, beautiful mind you run away from like the plague...

BENITO: Guess I hallucinated all the nights we had: taking long baths, playing cards with our friends, and you're drinking beers, telling dirty jokes, your hand on my knee, big, big laughter—

GABRIELA: We were drunk half the time!

BENITO: You told me you wanted eight kids with me.

GABRIELA: I thought I did.

BENITO: You didn't *think* you *did*, you did. Looked me in the eye. Sometimes the tears falling, fat as snakes, your fingers around my stick so tight you almost broke it, eyes on fire, you whisper so low and sexy: "I love you, baby," —you said that! — "so much, I want to have eight kids with you." The pants come down. The legs get wrapped around my neck. Do I not-believe that now? Was it a lie? Are you lying now? Were you crazy then? Are you crazy now?

GABRIELA: I was eighteen when I said that about the babies. With a big mouth and dreams. Long before we knew I was fixed and God was playing tricks with my body. Before the war changed you.

BENITO: The war didn't change me. It changed you.

GABRIELA: Fucking right it changed me. Every single day for a year...glued like a mummy to the T V... watching C N N, looking at all the American soldiers— going, "is that him? Is he eating okay? Does he look happy? No, it's not him. I don't see him. Don't see my Benito." So I turn the T V off and lie on the floor—and

imagine you naked in the desert...captured by the
enemy...no, no, they don't kill you right away, they
take their time...until you scream out your mother's
name when they've found your softest places and
learned how to take you apart and put you back
together any old way they fucking feel like it. And me
waiting, sucking in rumors like life-saving air: washing
dishes, cleaning, polishing the car, reading, pacing,
smoking, crying, punching holes in the walls, puking.

BENITO: High maintenance.

GABRIELA: I hated falling asleep 'cause of the dreams.
In my dream: I get your body after the war. You can't
move. I can't figure out why. You open your mouth
for me. I put my hand down your throat. My whole
arm goes in. Your skin is see-thru so I watch my hand
groping the things in your stomach. There's little
round rocks in you, smooth, like from a beach, and I
pull these outta your stomach by the fistful but you
don't get better. Not 'til I'm reaching deeper in your
bowels and pull out the rusted nails and burning bits
of shrapnel that were in there and they cut my hand to
pieces but I don't stop until I pull them all out of your
body.

(Beat)

BENITO: Do I get better?

GABRIELA: Never know. I wake up.

BENITO: Don't wanna end up married to a cripple, who
could blame you...?

GABRIELA: No, *mi cielo.* If you came home that way—I'd
take care of you. For the rest of your life. No questions
asked. But it has to be *you.* The man I met and loved...

BENITO: *(Losing his patience)* Christ, Gab, you make
it sound like the war's turned me into some kind of
animal. Look at these hands. They don't just pull

triggers and evaporate life. They have other jobs besides counting dead. These are good hands. You know that from experience. You know I can fix every bad dream in your head. I can cure this insanity you have...

GABRIELA: What if I can't? What if I can't get the dead women and children off your hands? What if I feel them every time you touch me?

BENITO: *Nena, Dios,* that's fucked what you're saying—

GABRIELA: It's gotta be said—I gotta know: are you inside there? All you did was come home from work. Me? I'm digging up my husband from the grave— looking for the lover I had before the world sucked out his mind and heart...

BENITO: You don't deserve to have a house. You don't deserve security.

GABRIELA: *Coño,* that is so lame it's not even ---

BENITO: Oh fuck it, fuck it! Man, what is wrong with me? Standing in this bedroom begging you to stay with me? I don't have to beg no damn woman for no damn thing in the world. You have decided—before I even got home. So great. So that's the message handed down from the Supreme Court, on the day of my return from busting my hump for her, the day of reunion, the day of new honeymoons and second chances. You've *assaulted* me with this shit. You've hit me right between the eyes, *nena.* It'd be better to just take my sidearm and let the bullets do the talking. I don't beg. A man does not beg. You go find what you're missing. Read every book in the world. 'Cause right now we're "like" oil and water, we're "like" a train wreck, and you know what? Thank you, baby. This was good. Saved us a lot of time. I now have more time to watch T V. *(He puts on clothes.)*

GABRIELA: What are you doing?

BENITO: You know what? You're wrong—I don't run from my mind, I don't, I live inside myself, where there's no way out, and I see what I do. I see what I put you through, for years.

GABRIELA: Could this be a whiff of a hint of a shadow of saying "I understand?"

BENITO: Just, please, hold on until I can retire in nine years. You can do it, Private. The war was a fluke. There will not be another one in my life. I'll do everything I can to get orders for anyplace on earth but Germany or the desert. I'll volunteer for Star Wars. I'll suck off the captain. I'll learn to type. Just don't make me rip my life in half and erase eleven years of it 'cause then I'm dead for sure, Gabby. *(He has to keep from crying. He pushes his emotions down, way down.)*

GABRIELA: Why do you gotta be so convoluted?

BENITO: 'Cause I'm not supposed to make it easy for you to break my heart.

GABRIELA: Like I made it easy for you?

BENITO: I'm gone. I'll be on post. You decide if you wanna be here when I come home tomorrow morning. We'll try the homecoming again, if you want. But really think about it. Think about me. Don't do anything until you think about me.

(BENITO leaves the room.)

(GABRIELA collapses into bed and thinks about everything.)

(Distant COYOTES howl.)

(GABRIELA falls asleep.)

(Blackout)

END OF ACT THREE

ACT FOUR

(Early morning. The backyard. A hint of sunlight over the east threatens the darkness.)

(The MOON *is faint, weak, low in the sky, softly playing the violin.)*

(The COYOTE's GHOST *and the* CAT *stare at each other in wonder.)*

*(*MARTIN *and* GABRIELA, *not touching, sleep side-by-side.)*

*(*GABRIELA *wears sweatpants and sweatshirt.)*

CAT: *(To the* COYOTE's GHOST) I thought you were dead, Coyote.

COYOTE'S GHOST: *(To the* CAT) I'm a ghost.

CAT: I thought I'd never see you again.

COYOTE'S GHOST: I'm a memory.

CAT: A vivid one—my heart remembers!
A difficult one too.

COYOTE'S GHOST: I'm a dream.
I'm not really here.

CAT: I know. I miss you.

COYOTE'S GHOST: You were right not to trust me.
I wanted to hurt you.
To teach you to be wild.
Then kill you quick—

and eat you
and not give a shit.

CAT: Then the moonlight stabbed you
and ripped you off,
and there was nothing
I could do about it.
And with your passing,
all my hopes for a wild ride
in the endless night seemed to end.
But you're back!

COYOTE'S GHOST: Am I?

CAT: I don't have to miss you anymore.

COYOTE'S GHOST: Why do you stare at me?

CAT: You're transparent!
It's so cool!

COYOTE'S GHOST: I can't even smell you.

CAT: Coyote, I'm hot.

COYOTE'S GHOST: I can't smell anything.
What kind of hunter will I be?

CAT: Smell me and you'll know.

COYOTE'S GHOST: My appetite for blood: gone!

CAT: There are other kinds of smells.
Other kinds of hunger.
An infinity of tastes.
And ways to satisfy.

COYOTE'S GHOST: What are you thinking, Cat?

CAT: Thoughts! Wild ones!
(She yowls in grief and heat.)

(MARTIN wakes up.)

MARTIN: *(To the MOON)*
After my pistol of love
found its target and

exploded with love-shrapnel
inside her, and sent her mind
to the dizzy edge of the universe,
where it sat and wondered
what the fuck hit it...
she fell asleep.
Mission accomplished!
I am now a man.
Seeds are planted.
Other men notice my manhood
and are suddenly afraid.

MOON: *(Bored, sarcastic)*
...So hide your daughters, people.

MARTIN: So hide your daughters, people!

(GABRIELA wakes up.)

GABRIELA: I just had the strangest dream...

MARTIN: I think I got you pregnant.

GABRIELA: Then you have the only sperm
on earth that crawls across cement,
burrows through cotton panties,
and grows flowers in barren sand.

MARTIN: Ask the moon what I did!

MOON: *(Weak)*
At night, love can't
hide from me.
My light penetrates.
When virgin blood and
virgin seed hit the sheets,
I'm there,
counting the droplets.
Last night? Zero.

GABRIELA: *(To the MOON)*
Delightful job you have.

MOON: *(Weak)*
It's a living.
But, now, my time is almost over.
Gotta go to bed.
My sister the sun is
impatient and pushy.

GABRIELA: In my dream: cats don't talk.
Refrigerators are indoor appliances.
The moon doesn't play the violin.
On the moon, sunlight cooks the land
and there's zero romance and no sound.
Dreams don't get born there.
Some day the moon will be landfill,
people think.
So the moon watches,
with indifference,
as the earth rises
out of its bleached horizon,
all soft and blue,
like a marble covered in tears.

(The MOON *yawns, gets dimmer.)*

MOON: Yeah, whatever.

GABRIELA: But what if I'm still dreaming?
What if none of us wake up?
What if we go on like this:
dreaming and sleeping, dreaming and sleeping,
until we're like boxes-within-boxes
and there's no way out?

MOON: *Adios,* Gabby!

GABRIELA: *(To the* MOON*)*
Before you go, explain my dream.
I couldn't recognize Benito and me.

MOON: It's a dream about soulmates.

GABRIELA: Who never agree? Who misinterpret?

MOON: You two go deep.
So the wounds go deep.
You give a person so much,
you rearrange them.
You re-write them.
He's your creation.
You're his.

GABRIELA: Was it all a mistake?
Was it all hormones
and sweaty fingers?
Beer and pot and sucking each other?
Was it the uniform?
Was it the jokes he told
and the food he cooked?
Was it just youth?
Why didn't I take more pictures
of those days?
Why can't I remember
them better?

MOON: *(Weak)*
Too tired to think...

GABRIELA: My parents went from one island,
Puerto Rico, to another island, Long.
They bought a little house
and never left it.
No interest in the horizon beyond.
I was losing my mind,
so I stole beer and blouses
from local establishments.
My desperate Mami
shipped me to cousins
in South Carolina
where I ran wild,
sneaking into all the bars,
looking for the lucky young man

to donate my cherry to.
Do you remember how me met?

MOON: A white trash bar.
A wild October night.
A melee.

GABRIELA: Fists flying, American GIs,
drunken rednecks.
Benito and other
Puerto Rican recruits
on the floor getting nailed
by local skinheads.
I pulled him to his feet
and ran out of the bar with him
before it got really ugly.
Saved him. Held him.
Brought him back to his own body.
To his future—and as far from his virginity
as he could get.
I was fifteen years old.
Our futures mingled—
it was sweet and reckless...
we were each other's
drugs and cigarettes...
we floated in and out of dreams
that both of us wrote...
wide-eyed, breathing fast,
hands like fish,
enough soft skin to cover
the earth ten times over,
turning from solid to liquid,
many liquids, many smells,
no waking up, ever.

MOON: *(Fading)*
...fading...

GABRIELA: Who wouldn't get married
under those circumstances?
Who wouldn't assume
that passion—and tenderness—
could last forever?
Who could have predicted
the changes in the body and the spirit?

(The MOON *starts to set.)*

MOON: *(Fading)*
...don't turn to me
for precise answers, Gabby...
I'm a reflection of a reflection...
I'm a co-dependent satellite...
not even confident enough
to be a planet...
and what you ask about
are intangibles...
there will always be things
you can't know about each other...
there has never been a machine
made to X-ray the heart
and reveal its secrets,
except for poetry...
and I'm way too tired
to deal with poetry tonight...
Shakespeare called me inconstant...
"that monthly changes in *her* circled orb"...
even got my gender wrong...
the motherfucker...
but I guess I am...
that's as close to precise
as the moon can get...

MARTIN: *(To the* MOON*)*
I wish you'd leave already!

MOON: *(To* GABRIELA*)*

...everything you do
will seem like a mistake...
for a very long time to come...

(Using his telescope like a gun, MARTIN takes aim at the MOON.)

MARTIN: Bang!

(The MOON disappears. More sunlight.)

GABRIELA: *(To MARTIN)*
Boy, you need to go.

MARTIN: But I'm your man.
And you stole my virginity.
You owe me something for that.

GABRIELA: Sun's coming up.
Benito comes home from the field
this morning, seven a.m.,
must be close to that,
I suggest you disappear, *muchacho*.

MARTIN: I'm only saying
I want to spoil you—
on a cellular level.

GABRIELA: Child, I'd break you in two.

MARTIN: Then give me back my virginity.

GABRIELA: I'll give you back your virginity.

(GABRIELA kisses MARTIN passionately.)

MARTIN: The giving was better than the taking!

GABRIELA: You're a sweet kid, Martin.
You don't belong in Barstow, either.
We have that in common.
You kiss good.

MARTIN: *(To the CAT)*
I kiss good!

GABRIELA: I could get into visiting you
every afternoon after school
and distracting you
from your math homework
and totally messing up your chances
for college.
I can see going crazy in your bed
and burning your house to the ground
with the two of us
taking long baths together
and drinking so much beer
we'd both have comas for a week.

MARTIN: I'm searching for the downside
to all this.

GABRIELA: I can see you getting
more and more dangerous, Martin.
I can tell by looking in your eyes:
you're the type
that falls in love real easy.
That plans babies
after the first conversation.
Like somebody I
fell in love with
when I wasn't much
older than you.

MARTIN: You think...other girls
see the same danger as you?

GABRIELA: You broadcast it through your eyes.

MARTIN: Are you saying I'll never get laid?

GABRIELA: Not with me, *muchachito.*

(MARTIN *looks at* GABRIELA, *angry, it's like his entire
personality has changed.*)

MARTIN: I gotta go.
There's nothing here.

Nothing here I want.
You hear me?
Nothing here I want!
Nothing here I want!

GABRIELA: Take it easy, Private...

MARTIN: This whole thing is bullshit!
And I don't want any more of you
playing with my head,
you cutting my nuts off,
you doing psycho-*brujeria*-witchcraft on me.
I'm glad we never got involved, bitch!
I'm glad I broke your heart!

GABRIELA: Did I miss something here...?

(MARTIN *starts to go over the fence.*)

MARTIN: This is my life:
I rent porn.
I shoot coyotes at night.
I harass faggots.
I steal my father's weapons.
I take target practice on the moon.
My accurate shots add
new craters every night.
But you made me think new thoughts!
And every day I get
closer and closer to manhood
and I worry how the world will crush me—
and if I don't touch a woman's thing,
like real soon,
will I finally go berserk
and blow you all away?
Or will my explosions
happen so deep inside
no one will feel them but me?

(MARTIN *is gone.*)

(GABRIELA *sadly thinks about him, the* MOON, *and* BENITO:
all the men of her life.)

(*The* CAT *looks at her, worried.*)

CAT: *(To* GABRIELA)
What are you going to do today?

GABRIELA:
Today I'm going to have both
my eyes sucked out of my face
and replaced with the eyes
of a teenage Persian slave girl.

CAT: Cool.

GABRIELA: I will grow some fruit today
in my womb.
I will recite the Holy Koran.
I will change into
Salvador Dali's foreskin
and fuck a red-haired soprano.
I will collect severed egos.
I will organize the red ants
that live in the garage and
teach them to milk each other
so I never run out of milk
for Benito's coffee.
I will melt time.
I will call Muhammad collect
and gossip about his homeboy Jesus.
I will drink a hummingbird's saliva
drop by little drop
and stare into Benito's eyes
and try to read his mind
and wonder if we still
love each other.
And if I can't figure it out
I think the thing I have to do
is devise a gruesome test.

CAT: A gruesome test! I like that!

GABRIELA: The first night we met,
as we ran from the bar and the cops,
into the night...
there was a wicked moon in the sky,
smoking a Cuban cigar,
playing a mandolin with
thirteen-and-a-half strings.
Benito stopped to look at the moon.
The skinheads were gaining on us.
He said it looked so cool tonight.
I didn't even notice it
and he made me notice it.
I realized I like a man who notices
the moon even with skinheads
coming closer and closer.
I thought that was brave and thoughtful.
I thought that was manly and kind.
He asked me if I was an angel.
He wondered if God would let him fuck me
if he was extra good around Christmas.
I was fifteen years old!
I can deal with anything if I know for sure
he's the same man I saved from peril.
So I'll ask him about last night.
Did he see last night's moon
or has he stopped looking
at the sky forever?

(The sound of a car entering the house's garage.)

CAT: Guess who.

(GABRIELA opens the refrigerator. It's full of sand.)

GABRIELA: *(Nervous)*
Outta milk!
I'm getting weird déjà vu.

Got nothing to wear
but cut-offs.

CAT: He'll see you like that
and think: horny housewife.

GABRIELA: This can't be like other times.
I have to think about Benito.
I have to make him see
we could be looking
at a train wreck...

(GABRIELA *starts to exit into the house.*)

CAT: *Nena*, wait! What do I do
if my lover's a ghost?

GABRIELA: Fuck him anyway, Cat.

(GABRIELA *enters the house.*)

(*The* COYOTE'S GHOST *and the* CAT *look at each other.*)

COYOTE'S GHOST: Do you trust me?

(*The* CAT *approaches the* COYOTE'S GHOST *and breathes deep.*)

CAT: Ay! You smell like air!
You smell—like heaven,
like a graveyard on a cloudy day.
You smell like transformation, hope, prayers.
You smell like a whisper.
Let's do something right now!

COYOTE'S GHOST: How long will I last with you?

CAT: Before we lose our courage?

COYOTE'S GHOST: How long do I really have?

CAT: Before the deceptions start?

COYOTE'S GHOST: And the fights to the death.

CAT: And the madness.

COYOTE'S GHOST: How long can we possibly last?

CAT: Before we have to test
each other's love?

(*The* CAT *and the* COYOTE'S GHOST *approach each other.*)

(*The* CAT *dances with the* COYOTE'S GHOST.)

(BENITO *enters, carrying duffle bags.*)

(GABRIELA *enters, wearing cut-offs and tank top.*)

BENITO: Where were you?

GABRIELA: I was in the backyard.
I slept there last night.

BENITO: Something wrong with the bed?

GABRIELA: I just did, that's all.

BENITO: Is there any coffee?

GABRIELA: You lost a lot of weight.

BENITO: God bless that Army food.

GABRIELA: And nice circles under the eyes.

BENITO: Ain't slept in forty-eight hours.

GABRIELA: You don't like my haircut...

BENITO: Makes you look older—
but not too much—
five or six years at the most!

GABRIELA: Here's your gun.

BENITO: Don't say "gun" —it's a "weapon."
Your gun hangs between your legs.

GABRIELA:
Nothing hangs between my legs, soldier-boy.

BENITO: Except for me. Gabby.
My cute, smart, sexy,
totally hot Gabby...

GABRIELA: I have a question.
It's going to sound stupid,

but I have to ask you.
Did you see the moon last night?

BENITO: ...better than pogey-bait...

GABRIELA: Did you see the moon last night?
I really have to know this, Benito.
I really have to know.

(Lights to black as GABRIELA *awaits* BENITO's *answer.)*

(The CAT *and the* COYOTE'S GHOST *dance slow and hot and tight.)*

END OF PLAY

CPSIA information can be obtained
at www.ICGtesting.com
Printed in the USA
LVHW041116301218
602197LV00016B/595